Using the Bible for Reading Out Loud

Clifford Warne and Paul White
Illustrated by Annie Vallotton

Series editor:
Wendy S. Robins

Bible Society

First published by The Anglican Information Office, Sydney,
Australia. June 1979
©Clifford Warne
Illustrations© Anglican Information Office
This Edition© BFBS 1980 10m
The Bible text in this book is taken from the Good News Bible
published by the Bible Societies/Collins
©American Bible Society, New York, 1966, 1971, 1976
Also from the Authorised Version, the Revised Standard
Version and the New English Bible.

This publication by the Bible Society,
146 Queen Victoria Street, London EC4V 4BX

ISBN 0 564 00950 4

Preface

Possibly because there are so many poor readers and speakers, people believe that the occasional good reader is just a person with a special gift. That is not the case. To be able to read aloud, sound natural and make the meaning clear is something which can be learned. The clues are in this book. They have been tried, tested and taught for many years by the authors, themselves master story tellers and effective readers.

The clear layout, numerous examples and brilliant illustrations by Annie Vallotton, highlight the text.

Having used and taught the logical principles contained in ''For Reading Out Loud'' I thoroughly recommend it to all who are serious about communicating the spoken word.

Philip N. Oliver
Director
A.I.O., Sydney

The Authors

Clifford Warne is both an author and entertainer with over 23 years experience in commercial television. He is currently Director of Anglican Television Productions in Sydney. Clifford Warne writes and lectures widely on the subject of speech communication.

Paul White, known by all as the Jungle Doctor, is the author of over 47 books. These have been published in more than 70 languages. Dr. White also exercises a world-wide ministry in radio and television.

Annie Vallotton is perhaps best known for her illustrations in the Good News Bible. In this book she combines with Paul White and Clifford Warne to add her own special and imaginative visual dimension.

Contents

Introduction to the British Edition

More people hear the Bible being read out loud than ever read it for themselves. They are the "hearers" of the Word of God, that we wish would become "doers" of it. They *hear* the lessons read in school assembly or R.E. class. They *hear* the Scripture readings at christenings, weddings and funerals. They *hear* the passages selected for parade services. They *hear* the Old Testament, Epistle, Gospel and Psalm in the Liturgy or at morning or evening prayer. They *hear* the Bible read at national ceremonies, broadcast on radio or television. In these days of joint liturgical lectionaries they *hear* groups and sequences of lessons that have truth in them well enough arranged to convert, educate and inspire thousands. Yet few are inspired, less are educated and hardly any ever converted by this battery of truth that they physically hear. It would seem that it goes in one ear and out of the other.

Why is this? Why is such a great opportunity so unproductive? I believe it is because the exercise is not thought of as **hearing.** It is universally thought of and spoken about as Scripture Reading.

Ministers, priests and lay people who are chosen to read out loud from the Bible are usually people who read quite a lot and read easily. They are used to books. It is natural for them to keep thinking of the Scripture lesson as a reading rather than a hearing. So long as the message on the page is passing through their eyes to their brain, so that it is understood, they have no special need of skilfully spoken emphasis, phrasing and expression to make the meaning clear. They read for readers. This is demonstrated by the way churches encourage congregations to read the lesson in their Bible or in an order of service along with the reader. The fact that many people will only grasp the meaning if they *hear* it with their ears without ever following it in print is not noticed.

This book could change that. It concentrates on how the Bible is heard when it is read out loud and gives practical help to make sure its meaning comes across clearly. It should be read and studied by every minister and priest. It should be sold, given or loaned to everyone who reads lessons in church, school or other functions. If this were done on a wide scale it could lead to more people really being confronted by the Word of God than any other single step we could take.

The book can obviously be used privately by individuals. Its value and impact will be greatly increased if its ideas are worked at in twos and threes so that there is at least one hearer at any practice in reading. Mutual encouragement can only be good, and being willing to receive help in reading God's Word more effectively will itself be a step towards personal growth. It could also lead to using more than one voice for some readings.

Some of the best ideas are very simple. The idea behind this book is one of them. It is that at no extra cost we could communicate the Word of God to thousands by doing better what they expect us to do anyway.

Tom Houston
Executive Director
Bible Society

Abbreviations

In this book we have used a number of abbreviations. Here's what they mean.

AV   Authorised Version of the Bible
RSV   Revised Standard Version of the Bible
NEB   New English Bible
GNB   Good News Bible
AIO   Anglican Information Office, Sydney, Australia
Lion Lion Publishing, Icknield Way, Tring, Herts.

Antonio Stradivari, the famous maker of violins, instructed his craftsmen, "No violin leaves this workshop until it is as close to perfection as human skill and care can make it."

If you could afford to buy a Stradivarius you would realize the standard of perfection they reached.

When Stradivari was asked, "Why this passion for perfection?" he had only one answer, "God needs violins to take his music to the world, and if my violins are defective God's music is spoiled."

These days God needs readers to take his word to the ears of the world and if our reading is defective God's word is spoiled.

1 For Reading Out Loud

Some people who think the Bible has *nothing* to say to them, do so not because they've read it, but because they've only heard it read.

An unprepared or careless reading of God's Book meant to them blurring of meaning and boredom.

These are days of trained news readers on television and radio. Why should we not have skilful Bible readers in church?

For the reader, learning, using and mastering the few rules set out in this book will make the Scriptures live in a new way.

For those who listen it can mean a new understanding of the Bible and a desire to read it for themselves.

The heart of the matter in reading aloud is:
To understand what you read
To sound natural
To make the meaning clear

When words are spoken, the *meaning* is not in the words alone, but in:
The emphasis
The phrasing
The expression given to those words

Understand what you read

"Will you please read the New Testament tonight?" is a common enough request.

This can merely mean a rapid read-through to make sure there are no unpronounceable names and a book mark in your Bible to find the place later.

Actually in being asked to read you have been given a splendid chance to voice God's word to people; of passing on his words that can change lives and influence the conduct of those who hear.

Listeners will either lose interest as your voice drones on, or they will sit up and take notice as God's word comes to them clearly, expressively and understandably. This can and will happen when you understand what you are reading and grasp the simple technique of making printed words ring in the ear and glow in the mind.

But doing this takes know-how and time.

You must give the time.

The know-how is in the pages that follow.

Read the portion of scripture you have been given, carefully.

Make sure you understand and grasp all the ideas behind the words, then mark for emphasis the words that bring out those ideas.

In preparation a hasty read-through is not enough. It is irresponsible handling of God's own book.

Meaning matters most.

Why do some readers emphasize wrong words, pause in wrong places and use the wrong expression?

Because **they don't understand fully what they read.**

If you wish to read aloud, sound natural and make the meaning clear.

See it, understand it and say it correctly.

Otherwise, what you **see** as you read is the word of God, but what you read aloud, what you **say,** is **not necessarily** the word of God.

Above all else it is the meaning that matters

Each sentence needs to be examined closely for meaning.

Preparation is essential; you cannot make up your mind in the split second when your eye takes in the line you are reading. For instance — What did Paul mean when he wrote, ''We preach Christ to all men''?

Six words and you have four possibilities.

1. ''*We* preach Christ to all men'' — Contrasting himself with others.

2. ''We preach *Christ* to all men'' — Was Paul telling about the subject?

3. Did he say, "We preach Christ to *all* men"? — Like John Wesley saying "The whole world is my parish".

4. Or did he say: "We preach Christ to all *men*"? — We're the Men's Society and we don't talk to women and children!

Unless you understand the idea in the passage to be read, you can't emphasize the right words.

Make yourself familiar with the text both before and after the portion you are to read. This gives you a much wider view.

You will be wise to have on your shelf the Bible in several translations. Paraphrases are useful. They can give the additional information which is not always seen in the text. This may help you to understand the meaning in order to make it clear to others.

Don't read aloud to others until you yourself understand the page before you. Incomplete understanding of what you read, no matter how warm your voice, polished your accent, or skilled your diction, takes most of the value out of your communication.

Translation of the Bible and Bible helps

Choose the translation which best fits the age of the audience, their grip on the language, and their spiritual understanding.

The Amplified Bible gives alternate meaning of words and is often helpful when you need to consult another version during preparation.

A Commentary and a Bible Dictionary are important. It is essential to understand technical words such as repentance, justification and righteousness. The New Bible Dictionary (IVP) and the New Bible Commentary (IVP), are excellent for the purpose.

Before you read have clearly in your mind:
Where are the events happening? The Photo Guides to the Old and New Testament (Lion) are recommended.
When do the events take place?
Who are the people involved?
How do they act and react?
Why do they act and react as they do?

This is so important that we say it again:

It is the meaning that matters.

Understand what you read.

Know all the ideas in the text.

Then emphasize the words that bring out these ideas. For the meaning of spoken words is made clear when you emphasize the words which bring out the true meaning of the text.

2

Emphasis

Stress on certain words is emphasis. In the language of the news reader you *hit* these words. If you emphasize the wrong word, you will cloud, confuse or, even worse, change the meaning of the text.

The church was full. An enthusiastic young man offered to read the first lesson. 1 Kings 13 was written on the slip of paper handed to him. He ran his eye over the chapter.

Later as he read aloud he wondered at the sound of subdued laughter as he read. "He said, 'Saddle *me* the ass'. So they saddled *him* the ass." He was not aware that he had made an ass of himself.

How different it would have been if he had read, "*Saddle* me the *ass*, so they *saddled* him the ass."

Recently at a communion service the minister kept on emphasizing the pronoun in the commandments:

You shall not commit adultery.

You shall not steal.

You shall not commit murder.

He should have read:

You shall *not* commit *adultery*.

You shall *not steal*.

You shall *not* commit *murder*.

The emphasis *must* be on the *right* words

A beautifully modulated voice on the radio read, "He loved the *good* things of this life."

And why shouldn't we all love the "*good*" things of this life?

What we were meant to understand was, "He loved the good things of *this* life," conveying the idea that he preferred not the spiritual life but the earthly one.

This gives a very different meaning.

You may well ask, "Shouldn't the audience make out the meaning for themselves?"

The moment people start asking themselves, "What was that?" or "What did he say?" they miss the next sentence and lose the thread of the reading. The audience thinks many times faster than the reader speaks. Distraction makes the mind stray from the thought track.

Change emphasis and you change meaning

Emphasis can lead up a variety of paths. For instance here is a sentence: "All the girls like Peter."

If you put the accent on "*all*", you're saying every girl likes Peter.

If your emphasis is on "*girls*", you imply the boys don't.

If you read, "All the girls *like* Peter", you're assuring us of their attitude to Peter.

If you emphasize "*Peter*", you're saying that he is preferred to others.

Thus by changing emphasis you change meaning.

A reading with *incorrect emphasis* is like a poorly tuned radio. The sound is confused and muddled. It is possible to work out the tune but it is a struggle to appreciate the harmony

Meaning comes through emphasis.

Wrong emphasis hides meaning.

Wrong emphasis *changes* meaning.

Rule 1
Emphasize those words which introduce each new idea

First, understand what the text says. See *all* the ideas in the text.

Find the **meaning** words, the words that bring out each idea.

These **meaning** words have a gong inside them. Hit these words and they ring. Hit the others and there is only a dull thud.

Look at John 1.1, "In the *beginning* was the *Word*. The Word was *with God*, the Word *was* God."

The new ideas in the first phrase are "*the Word*", and the Word existing from "the *beginning*." In the second, "*with God*" is the new idea. In the third, the new idea is "*was* God."

"You will be ready to suffer with me for the Lord, for he will give you strength in suffering."

In the second half of the sentence "in suffering" is the old idea. Subdue it. "He will *give* you *strength*" is the new idea. Stress it. Emphasis is not put on "in suffering" because it is an old idea.

Rule 1 Exercise
Key to exercises begins on page 43

Emphasize new ideas:

Try these examples.

A. John made a model of St. Paul's Cathedral. He made the model in five days.

B. Be persistent in prayer, and keep alert as you pray.

C. In all my prayers for you, I always pray with joy; and I never give up praying for you.

D. Sanctify them by the truth; your word is truth.

E. Love is patient; love is kind and envies no one. Love is never boastful, nor conceited, nor rude.

F. All that the Father gives me will come to me; and whoever comes to me I will never drive away.

G. By calling God his own Father, he claimed equality with God.

You will now recognize what are new ideas and will emphasize them.

Rule 2
Soft pedal old ideas

Don't emphasize old ideas mentioned earlier. Old ideas may have been mentioned three or four sentences before, or even further back. Old ideas are *not* to be emphasized.

"In these colonnades there lay a crowd of sick people, blind, lame, and paralysed. Among them was a man who had been crippled for thirty-eight years. When Jesus *saw* him lying there and was *aware* that he had been ill a long time, he asked him, 'Do you want to recover?' "

You would not emphasize "lying there" or "he had been ill for a long time." The new ideas are "when Jesus *saw* him . . . and was *aware* . . ."

Rule 2 Exercise

Don't emphasize old ideas which were mentioned earlier in the text:

A. Thomas said to him, "Lord, we do not know where you are going; how can we know the way to get there?" Jesus said to him, "I am the way, and the truth, and the life."

B. "It is my Father who gives you the real bread from heaven. For the bread that God gives is he who comes down from heaven and gives life to the world." "Sir," they asked him, "give us this bread always." "I am the bread of life," Jesus told them.

Rule 3
Be careful of synonyms. You don't emphasize old ideas, even when they're dressed up in new words

Different words may still express an old idea and therefore must be played down.

"He gave up chocolate and ice cream, and tried hard to avoid eating all kinds of sweets."

As chocolate and ice cream are kinds of sweets we don't emphasize *kinds of sweets* but *all*. That's the new idea. We would emphasize "tried hard" but subdue "to avoid eating" as it's an old idea expressed in "gave up".

"Have you seen inside the Cathedral? It's a beautiful place of worship."

Cathedral is a place of worship, *beautiful* is the new idea. Stress "beautiful". Subdue "place of worship."

"I wasn't interested in buying the clock. I thought he was asking too much for such an ancient time-piece."

A clock is a time-piece therefore don't emphasize an old idea in new words. Stress "ancient". Subdue "time-piece".

Rule 3 Exercise

Don't emphasize synonyms (old ideas dressed up in new words or phrases):

But you do not live as your human nature tells you to; instead, you live as the Spirit tells you to — if, in fact, God's Spirit lives in you. Whoever does not have the Spirit of Christ does not belong to him. But if Christ lives in you, the Spirit is life for you because you have been put right with God, even though your bodies are going to die because of sin.

Rule 4
Emphasize words which make a contrast

Some words do more than tell us new ideas, they also make a contrast with an idea already expressed. Therefore emphasize them.

"*Hatred* provokes disputes. *Love* covers over all offences."
We emphasize "love" because it is in contrast with "hatred".

"To *feel sorry* for the needy is not the mark of a Christian, to *help* them is."
The contrast is between "feeling sorry" and "helping".

The Bible contains many examples of contrast. King Solomon produced hundreds in Proverbs and Ecclesiastes. As an exercise, try reading Proverbs Chapter 2.

Rule 4 Exercise

Emphasize words that make a contrast:

A. If it's difficult for a good man to be saved, what will become of sinful men?

B. Ask God to bless those who persecute you. Yes, ask him to bless, not curse.

19

Rule 5A and 5B
Watch for and emphasize double contrasts, and multiple contrasts

C. For our fight is not against any physical enemy. It is against organizations and powers which are spiritual.

D. There are two kinds of leaders: those interested in the flock and those interested in the fleece.

E. Never help an old lady across the street — escort her.

Sometimes a writer records more than one contrast. He may use a double contrast, when the first idea contrasts with the second, then a third idea contrasts with a fourth.

"*Righteousness* is the road to *life*; *wickedness* is the road to *death*."
   Contrast "righteousness" with "wickedness"; and "life" with "death".

"*Thoughtless* words can *wound* as deeply as any sword, but *wisely* spoken words can *heal*."
   Contrast "thoughtless" with "wisely"; and "wound" with "heal".

Writers also use **Multiple Contrasts** where the first idea contrasts with the second and the third with the fourth, the fifth with the sixth and so on.

"*Everyone* serves the *best* wine *first*, and waits until the guests have drunk freely before serving the *poorer* sort; but *you* have kept the best wine till *now*."
1st contrast: "Everyone" with "you".
2nd contrast: "Best" with "poorer".
3rd contrast: "First" with "now".

"The *wages* of *sin* is *death*, but the *gift* of *God* is *eternal life*."
1st contrast: "Wages" with "gift".
2nd contrast: "Sin" with "God".

3rd contrast: "Death" with "eternal life".

Now emphasize the multiple contrasts in the exercises.

Rule 5A Exercise

Watch for double contrasts. Emphasize words which make the contrasts:

A. It's the duty of government to make it difficult for people to do wrong, easy to do right.

B. For the message of Christ's death on the cross is nonsense to those who are being lost; but for those who are being saved, it is God's power.

C. I don't understand what I do. I don't do what I'd like to do, but instead I do what I hate.

D. If you forgive the sins of others, God will forgive you.

E. God resists the proud, but he gives grace to the humble.

Rule 5B Exercise

Watch for multiple contrasts. Emphasize the words which make the contrasts:

A. "So then, anyone who hears these words of mine and obeys them is like a wise man who built his house on rock. The rain poured down, the rivers overflowed, and the wind blew hard against that house. But it did not fall, because it was built on rock.
"But anyone who hears these words of mine and does not obey them is like a foolish man who built his house on sand. The rain poured down, the rivers overflowed, the wind blew hard against that house, and it fell. And what a terrible fall that was!"

B. I have come accredited by my Father, and you have no welcome for me; if another comes self-accredited you will welcome him.

Rule 6
Watch for and emphasize suggested contrasts

Sometimes the writer suggests a contrast when he only expresses half the contrast. How do you see a suggested contrast? The meaning makes the suggestion.

They said, "It has taken forty-six years to build this temple. Are you going to raise it again in three days?" But the temple *he* was speaking of was his body.
   Here we have a suggested contrast between the Temple *they* were speaking of and the Temple *he* was speaking of. So stress "*he*" suggesting a contrast with the unwritten "*they*".

"For the Scripture says: *I* will take revenge, *I* will pay back, says the Lord."
   The accent is on "I" both times because the Lord is saying, "Vengence is 'mine, not yours'. *You* don't take revenge — *I* do."

Rule 6 Exercise

Watch for suggested contrasts. Emphasize that word which suggests the contrast:

A. You must work, not for this perishable food, but for the food that lasts, the food of eternal life.

B. There is no difference in the Lord's sight between one day and a thousand years; to him the two are the same.

Rule 7
Stress the contrasting pronouns

Pronouns are substitutes for nouns so they are usually old ideas and as such should not generally be stressed. However, when the meaning calls for it they should be stressed. This occurs when they make a contrast.

Ask *her*, not *him*.

This is *mine*, not *yours*.

Let *us* sing, not *them*.

Rule 7 Exercise

Stress the contrasting pronouns:

A. I am the vine, you are the branches.

B. If we disown him, he also will disown us.

C. Just as I do not belong to the world, they do not belong to the world.

D. Keep them safe by the power of your name, so that they may be one as you and I are one.

E. I sent them into the world, just as you sent me into the world.

F. As he grows greater, I must grow less.

Any word you can leave out need not be emphasized.

When an adjective and noun come together, what do you emphasize? Whatever the meaning tells you to emphasize

He spoke to an *old man.*

He spoke to an *old* man. (Implies the man wasn't young.)

He spoke to an old *man.* (Implies the person wasn't a woman.)

So the meaning determines whether you emphasize both adjective and noun; or the adjective; or the noun.

But look at these examples:

He was a Chinese teacher.

He was a giant killer.

He was an antique lover.

Each of the previous statements can be read two ways. You could only know what to emphasize if you knew the meaning, and here we haven't enough information. So, first find the meaning, then emphasize the word or words that make the meaning clear.

Rule 8
When an adjective and noun come together, most often you emphasize the adjective because it describes the noun

I saw a *new* film called the *Poseidon* Adventure. *Next* week they're showing the *Lawless* Bunch.
Which Adventure? The *Poseidon* Adventure.
Which Week? *Next* week.
Which Bunch? The *Lawless* Bunch.

God has saved us and called us to live a **holy** life.
What kind of life? A *holy* life.

Live as **obedient** children before God.
What kind of children? *Obedient* children.

Rule 8 Exercise

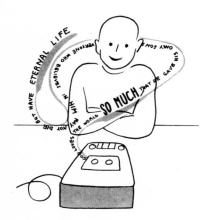

When an adjective and noun come together, most often you emphasize the adjective because it describes the noun:

A. Don't let your character be moulded by the desires of your ignorant days.

B. A raving beauty is the girl who came second in the beauty contest.

C. In the days when you were still pagan, you worshipped those dumb heathen gods.

D. Our old sinful nature is against God.

E. Any child raised by the book must be a first edition.

F. Here is a trustworthy saying.

Rule 9
Be careful of the word "thing" or "things". Emphasize the word or phrase which describes the thing

By itself, the word "thing" has no meaning. You find its meaning in the word or words which describe the thing. So, emphasize the word or phrase describing the thing. These are adjectives or adjectival phrases.

"The easiest thing is to find fault."
    Which thing? The *easiest* thing. So emphasize "easiest".

Now try the examples below.

Rule 9 Exercise

Beware of the word "thing":

A. He gave us his Son. Will he not also freely give us all things?

B. Don't touch unclean things.

C. Most folk pay too much for the things they get for nothing.

D. Away then with sinful earthly things! Deaden the evil desires lurking within you.

E. The wisest of us is a fool in some things.

F. Example is not the main thing in influencing others, it is the only thing.

G. By him all things were created; things in heaven and on earth.

H. After a man says "I do", he discovers a long list of things he'd better not do.

I. One nice thing about your enemies is that they don't try to borrow money from you.

J. One of the hardest things about business is minding your own.

Rule 10
Emphasize verbs when the meaning wants them emphasized

There is a strong temptation to say, "Ah, the verb, that's where the action is. Let's hit it."

If this is done, the voice starts to sound unnatural for this is rarely done in everyday conversation.

Only emphasize the verb when the meaning requires it to be emphasized.

For example: When it talks of something new or makes a contrast.

One occasion when emphasis is required is when the verb commands.

Jump on it! *Cut* the string! *Stop* that!

Rule 10 Exercise

Emphasize verbs when they command:

A. Close the door.

B. Repent! For the kingdom of heaven is at hand.

C. Obey your parents.

D. Leave the box there, and get the lid from Jim.

E. Go to mother, tell her Mrs. Smith has arrived and ask her for the parcel.

Rule 11
Don't stress "when"

Beware of over-emphasizing the word *when*. The question to ask yourself is, "when what?"

It is what follows *when* that is important.

In the phrase, "When they came to the other side of the lake," the emphasis is on "came" or on "other" not on "when".

Rule 11 Exercise

Don't stress "when":

A. When they came to the other side of the lake . . .

B. When Pilate saw that the crowd was getting out of hand . . .

C. When they realized the child was dead . . .

D. When they came to the tomb . . .

E. When he had taken the wine, he said . . .

Rule 12
Subdue words in parentheses

What is in parentheses can be left out without changing the meaning. Anything that can be left out without changing the meaning does not need to be emphasized.

On a road map the main road is shown as a thick strong line. Detours and side roads are mere dotted lines. The printer has emphasized the main road and played down the detour.

In reading out loud we emphasize the main road argument and subdue the extra bits of information.

Rule 12 Exercise

Subdue information in parentheses:

This information can be left out without affecting the main storyline or line of argument.

Information in parentheses might be enclosed in brackets, dashes, or commas. Subdue it.

A. Jesus said to him, "Go, wash in the pool of Siloam" (which means Sent). So he went and washed and came back seeing.

B. Thomas, called the Twin, said to his fellow disciples, "Let us also go, that we may die with him."

C. Nicodemus, who had gone to him before, and who was one of them, said to them, "Does our law judge a man without first giving him a hearing and learning what he does?"

Wrong emphasis *clouds* the meaning.

Wrong emphasis *confuses* the meaning.

Wrong emphasis *changes* the meaning.

A clergyman who heard this said, "You'd never believe it but every week in reading the service I emphasized different words. I thought if I did this I'd keep the words of the prayers and creed fresh. What a cloud I've blown over the meaning."

If a passage is read correctly the emphasis will always be the same because the meaning remains constant.

Wrong emphasis clouds the meaning.

Wrong emphasis confuses the meaning.

Wrong emphasis changes the meaning.

3 Phrasing and Pauses

Who has not heard a reader take a deep breath and then gallop through a reading at a speed that often leaves the listener's mind staggering.

What a relief to hear another who pauses to bring deeper meaning into his reading.

That valuable device, the pause, is a short period of silence following a word or a group of related words conveying a thought — a phrase.

A pause gives *the listener* the chance to understand and remember what he has just heard.

The reader has the double opportunity to breathe in quietly and to let his eye take in the words immediately ahead.

Look at John 3.16. If it is read in one breath the listener battles to grasp the meaning even though only the right words have been emphasized. The speed, together with absence of pauses, gives little opportunity for those magnificent words and ideas to register in the mind.

How different if you hear it this way. (The mark / indicates a pause.) God loved the world so much / that he gave his only Son, / that everyone who has faith in him / may not die / but have eternal life.

If the appropriate pause is made, each of these vital ideas has the opportunity to sink in.

An inexperienced or uninformed reader may pause wrongly and lose the whole impact and message of this tremendous verse.

A reader who had not prepared, read without any pause "And the shepherds came with haste and found Mary and Joseph and the baby lying in the manger."

The correct reading is "... and found Mary and Joseph / and the baby lying in the manger."

There is the uncomfortable story of a certain inept chairman who paused unwisely in his introduction of an after-dinner speaker, "And now I would like you to meet that well-known pest / extermination expert, Mr. Flip".

Pauses in the wrong places

Misplaced pauses can produce shudders. Try a pause before the last word of the sentence, "What's the dog chewing on Grandpa?"

Or more gruesome still, "What's that on the road ahead?"

There was the rather dreamy minister who remarked, "We had twenty odd people in church last Sunday". He would have saved himself many explanations if he had paused in the right place. (Pause *after* "odd".)

Pause in the wrong place or fail to pause in the right place and you'll cloud, confuse or change the meaning.

A group of related words, is called a *phrase*.

You group together the related words by pausing at the end of them.

A *pause* is a moment of silence following a word or phrase.

A. In my opinion / whatever we may have to go through now / is less than nothing / compared with the magnificent future God has in store for us.

B. In the light of the grace I have received / I want to urge each one among you, / not to exaggerate his real importance.

C. It is plain to anyone with eyes to see / that at the present time / all created life groans in a sort of universal travail.

D. We who have strong faith / ought to shoulder the burden of the doubts and qualms of the weak / and not to just go our own sweet way.

Marking your Bible to assist reading aloud

Don't hesitate to mark your Bible to guide your pausing and emphasis. Your memory can easily let you down.

Below is a practical way to mark up a passage for phrasing and pausing:

"I am the bread of life," / Jesus told them. / "He who comes to me will never be hungry; / he who believes in me will never be thirsty.

/ Now, I told you / that you have seen me but will not believe. // Everyone whom my Father gives me will come to me. / I will never turn away anyone who comes to me, / because I have come down from heaven / to do not my own will / but the will of him who sent me. / And it is the will of him who sent me / that I should not lose any of all those he has given me, / but that I should raise them all to life on the last day. / For what my Father wants is / that all who see the Son and believe in him / should have eternal life. / And I will raise them to life on the last day.''//

The people started grumbling . . .

Some find value in a large type copy of the Bible to make marking easier and more visible.

Watch the type of paper and pen used. If the ink is unduly absorbed difficulty may be experienced on reading overleaf.

Commas

Don't be mesmerized by commas. There is *no* rule that says you must pause at commas. Why? Because often the meaning of the text calls for a pause where there is no comma.

In John 3.16 the King James Version and the Revised Version have three commas. Only one is to be found in the Revised Standard Version, the Good News Bible, the Jerusalem Bible and the New English Bible. While J. B. Phillips puts in two!

''Where does the Bible say that children should be baptised?''

There are three possible meanings:

On which part of the body?

In which part of the church?

In which part of the Bible?

''Where does the Bible *say* that / *children* / should be baptised?''

Obviously, the meaning is — In which part of the Bible. Note: pauses needed before ''children'' and after ''children''.

The meaning, not commas, calls for the pauses.

There is *no* rule that says you must pause at commas because sometimes the meaning of a text does not want a pause where there *is* a comma.

"Whilst riding a ferry with Enrico Caruso, the entertainer, Al Jolson asked him would he appear with him on a concert program."

In his day Caruso was known as the world's greatest tenor. Jolson was known as the world's greatest entertainer. Although Caruso entertained his audience, in this context the word "entertainer" refers to Jolson. So you would pause between "Caruso" and "the entertainer", but you would not pause between "the entertainer" and "Al Jolson" — regardless of that second comma!

It is well known that you cannot always trust an author's punctuation be he Shakespeare or be she Agatha Christie.

In the original Greek of the New Testament there is no punctuation.

All this brings out the question, "What then is the value of punctuation if it doesn't tell you where to pause?"

Punctuation should assist in giving the meaning and you decide from the meaning where you will pause.

The meaning tells you where you should pause, not the punctuation.

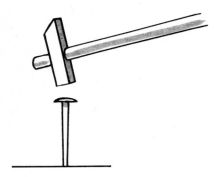

Wrong ideas about phrasing

Be warned about 2 wrong ideas

1. *No rule says:* The only place you need pause is at punctuation marks.

If there was no more to the art of reading than pausing at punctuation marks everyone would read well.

All they would need to do is pause at commas, colons, etc.

You will never make meaning clear doing this thoughtlessly.

2. *No rule says:* Pause at commas.

Why? For 3 reasons.

1. Sometimes long sentences don't have commas. You will need to pause during the sentence or expire!

Restricting phrases

2. You can't trust an author's punctuation.

Many good books have bad punctuation, even Bible translations.

"From Paul, a servant of Jesus Christ / who has been called to be an apostle."

Without a pause after Jesus Christ, Jesus is classified as an apostle. The reference of course is to Paul. So pause to separate "Jesus Christ" from "who has been called to be an apostle".

3. Often the meaning of the text wants a pause where there is no comma.

Often the meaning of the text does not want a pause where there is a comma.

A Restricting phrase restricts or limits the person or thing spoken about to being one particular person or thing.

A Restricting phrase is as essential to the meaning as a rock is to an oyster. The oyster is never the same again if you separate it from its rock.

The sense of the subject is spoiled if you separate subject from restricting phrase.

This comes into focus if you look into the sentence:

"The tiger with the circus clown in his mouth must be shot immediately."

There are six tigers in the cage. Which one must be shot?

The restricting phrase "with the circus clown in his mouth" makes it very clear what must be done by the man with the rifle.

With restricting phrases **do not pause** between subject and phrase. It is essential to the sense of the subject.

There is no place for commas in restricting phrases.

"The doctor with the knife in his hand will operate." Which doctor? Not the doctors in the gallery or those standing in the corner but "the doctor with the knife in his hand" is the one. There is no pause. You are quick to explain the situation.

The restricting phrase restricts the subject to being one particular person or thing.

A. God listens to men who are devout and do his will.

What kind of men? Men who are devout and do his will.

"Who are devout and do his will" restricts "men" to be of a particular kind.

B. If there is one of you who has not sinned let him be the first to cast a stone.

Which one of you? The one of you who has not sinned.

"Who has not sinned" restricts "one" to being a particular "one".

C. The man who enters by the gate is the Shepherd of the Sheep.

Which man? The man who enters by the gate.

"Who enters by the gate" restricts "the man" to being a particular man.

The restricting phrase is so essential to the sense of its subject you can't separate them!

So — don't pause before a restricting phrase.

A. The man in the moon is a myth.

B. No one serving as a soldier gets involved in civilian affairs.

C. It was works of this kind done on the Sabbath that stirred up the Jews to persecute Jesus.

D. Many a man who keeps out of trouble gets credit for a cool head when it's really cold feet.

Non-restricting phrases

A Non-restricting phrase does not limit its subject.

Read this sentence below noting that you pause before the non-restricting phrase, "in the straw hat".

"My wife, in the straw hat, planted those roses."

If you don't pause you're a bigamist; if you do you're reading correctly.

Non-restricting phrases need to be suitably supplied with

commas. If the author or printer has not used a comma before the non-restricting phrase you must see the meaning and still pause before the phrase.

"If you do not honour the Son, you do not honour the Father who sent him."

"Who sent him" is a non-restricting phrase. It does not restrict "the Father" to being one particular Father.

There is only one God the Father. "Who sent him" just adds information about the Father. It is a non-restricting phrase. So, pause before it!

The non-restricting phrase simply adds information about the subject.

Pause before a non-restricting phrase.

A. Stephen, who was full of grace and power, began to work great miracles and signs among the people.

B. Our Prime Minister, who speaks French, is visiting Paris.

C. And he came to Nazareth, where he was brought up.

D. The Sadducees, who say there is no resurrection, came to him with a question.

Check

In the matter of restricting phrases:

Leave it out of the sentence. If the meaning then is **not** clear, the phrase is a restricting one.

In the matter of non-restricting phrases:

Leave it out of the sentence. If the meaning is still clear, the phrase is Non-restricting.

The pause — a valuable tool

Actors and announcers use pauses to accomplish many things.

First and foremost a correctly placed pause makes meaning clear and helps the audience to grasp that meaning.

The skilled reader will use a pause to indicate a change of time or place.

A pause can also separate ideas.

A major use of the pause is to point to an idea in the text; to draw the audience's attention to a particular idea, pause before or after that idea.

To point to the subject of a sentence, pause after it.

To point to the action the subject takes, pause before the verb.

To point to the object, pause before it.

As well as **pausing, reduce pace** when speaking the key idea to which you're pointing.

Illustrations for pausing to point

A. I tell you the very truth, before the cock crows you will have denied me / three times!

B. And when he had exhausted every kind of temptation, the devil withdrew / until his next opportunity.

C. It is the shepherd of the flock / who goes in by the door.

D. I do assure you that / I myself / am the door for the sheep.

E. Now concerning / food offered to idols.

Theatre critics gave a French actor rave reviews for his roles in Molière's plays. They said, "He brought fresh life to these classics of the French theatre, his pausing was brilliant." That line made the actor glow with satisfaction. He said, "Ah, the words are Molière's but the pauses are mine."

What did he accomplish by pausing in the right place?

1. He made the meaning of the text clear and gave the audience the opportunity to register the meaning.

2. By his pausing he drew their attention to ideas and thoughts they might have missed.

4 Expression

Expression is the third key point in Reading Aloud. Expression is your tone of voice when you use words.

Do you speak with anger, or compassion?

Is there fear in your voice or pride or humility? It sounds in your expression.

How do you know what expression to use? The sense of the text should tell you.

When Paul is talking to the Philippians he talks with great joy; to the Galatians with disappointment; to Timothy he brings loving concern.

Expression can carry a wide variety of emotions.

In reading out loud try Matthew 22.23 and what follows. The Sadducees came to Jesus with the problem story of the seven brothers and the one wife. Their spokesman presented what sounded like a very serious proposition. As his argument built up he seemed to feel that he was doing very well. A smugness came into his voice. The Lord answered crisply, that he didn't know the power of God or the Scriptures and inferred he did not properly understand what Moses had written.

How do you get the right tone of voice into a reading of this situation?

It is not achieved by on-the-spur-of-the-moment reading, but calls for careful preparation, understanding and the use of all the principles, to give the meaning.

You then colour the words with careful expression. It is the sense that gives you the tone of voice.

Expression adds colour, warmth, depth, to words. The emphasis cannot be changed without changing the meaning. However, in expression there is wide scope for individuality with variation in pace, pitch and volume, but always in a normal not a "professional" voice. It is essential to sound natural.

Unusual voices distract and discourage people from listening.

The meaning comes in the expression.

There are a number of ways of saying, "Peter, put the cat out".

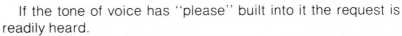

If the tone of voice has "please" built into it the request is readily heard.

The words can come with an imperative sound. Exasperation makes itself transparently clear.

What you *see* as you read is the word of God.

But when you read aloud, what you *say, is not necessarily* the word of God.

When you read the Bible with wrong emphasis, wrong phrasing or faulty expression you change the meaning or hide the meaning.

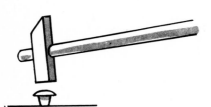

How do you know when to change expression or when to change volume, pace or pitch? The meaning of the text tells you.

Understand what you read.

Then read with a tone of voice that brings out the meaning.

Which meal would you choose?

It was to be a popular lecture by a world famous continental chef.

A wonderful aroma came from his kitchen. The audience leaned forwards expectantly as the dapper, smiling, culinary expert stepped onto the platform. Assistants carried a number of loaded trays.

With a flourish he announced, "The materials are the best and the cooking is of fine quality." He paused dramatically. "So far so good. But serving it . . . How important *that* is."

He whisked off a cover to display coarse china, chipped and smeary. Beside it was dull looking cutlery that spoke of sketchy washing in tepid water. Onto the unattractive plates he carelessly dumped the food.

Turning to his astonished audience, he shrugged, "This is *one* way of serving a notable meal."

A second cover was lifted. This time there was fine sparkling china. Knives gleamed, the silver of the spoons and forks shone. With care and artistry he served the meal.

The lecturer paused and smiled whimsically. "Ladies and Gentlemen, which meal would you choose?"

Meaningful expression

There is high importance in putting expression into meaning.

The precision tools are the big three:

Volume, Pace, Pitch.

Writers change feelings. Stories change moods.

The responsible reader will communicate these changes of mood and emotion. It is essential to give all the ideas meaningful expression.

The tone of voice used must fit the meaning of the words to be read. This is done through the use of the big three: volume, pace and pitch.

The reader speaks at a moderate volume, pace or pitch. When the story becomes exciting increase the "big three". If it becomes full of suspense decrease them.

Use them to show changes of time or place; also to distinguish narration from dialogue.

Understand the written words and read them with expression that fully brings out the meaning.

When Paul wrote to the Galatians he used clear, emotional, and intensely personal language.

The apostle does not write a cold theological treatise but a warm person-to-person letter full of loving concern tinged with some taut phrases. He is obviously deeply affected by their actions.

To read Galatians with unawareness or without appreciation of these built-in emotions, is to rob the listener of the true meaning of the epistle.

A man with an unsmiling face stood at the dimly-lit lectern of the large church. In the sing-song-not-ordinary voice many use in preaching, he read from the Bible. The congregation sat politely silent. The sonorous voice droned on. The listeners' attention was lost after the first few verses. His "reverent" but monotonous voice finished, "Here endeth the second lesson."

The reading was over — and forgotten.

The same words read as they are meant to be are living, powerful, surgically sharp and effective. But it means work.

Another man spent two hours preparing the chapter to be read. There was a glow inside him when he realized that the meaning of the passage was clearer in his mind than ever before.

He marked his Bible for emphasis and pauses, read the chapter, recording it on his cassette player and playing it back to himself. As he did this his pen marked one place where he had overlooked a contrast, another where a pause would make the meaning clearer.

In the church his face was relaxed in a smile, his eyes greeted his listeners as he told them the book and chapter from which he was reading. (He had checked the microphone before the service.)

People listened as he read clearly, enthusiastically in a normal voice. They heard, understood and appreciated as their ears and eyes were held by a reader who loved God and his word and prepared the reading as carefully as he would a talk.

5 When Reading Aloud

Keep your finger on the place.

Make sure the people at the back can hear.

Have someone there to signal to you should your voice fade.

Check the microphone — don't tap it, blow gently on it. — Make sure it is turned on.

Check your distance from the mike — generally a span.

Articulate words from your lips.

Listen to your practice reading on your cassette recorder. (You may not like what you hear! Don't blame the recorder.)

Reading to others, sounding natural, and making the meaning clear is easy — if you work at it. The clues are in this book. They'll work for you, if you work for them.

Owning a tool does not make you an expert, but using it produces results. The more you use it the better the results. The rewards go to those who persist.

Key to Exercises

This key draws attention to certain ideas in the exercises. Obviously there are other ideas in each text which must be emphasized: the answer below says, "Be sure you don't miss this one!"

If ever you are in doubt about emphasizing a word or phrase, read the sentence aloud leaving it out. If the meaning of the sentence is still clear without that word or phrase, then you don't need to emphasize it. That's a handy test! Words that can be left out don't need emphasis.

Page 17 1A In the second sentence emphasize the new idea "*five days*".

1B In the second half of the sentence emphasize the new idea "*keep alert*".

1C In the second half of the sentence emphasize the new ideas "*joy*" and "*never give up*".

1D In the second half of the sentence emphasize the new idea "*your word*".

1E In the second half of the first sentence emphasize the new ideas "*kind*" and "*envies no one*".
In the second sentence emphasize the new ideas "*never boastful, nor conceited, nor rude*".

1F In the second half of the sentence emphasize the new idea "*never drive away*".

1G In the second half of the sentence emphasize the new idea "*equality*".

Page 18 2A In Jesus' answer to Thomas, "way" is an old idea. Subdue it. Emphasize "*I*" as a new idea. Then emphasize "*truth*" and "*life*" as new ideas.

2B In Jesus' answer "bread of life" is an old idea. Subdue it. Emphasize "*I*" as the new idea.

Page 19 3A Once you have emphasized "*Spirit*" as a new idea, you subdue each mention of the Spirit even though it comes dressed up in a new name such as "God's Spirit", "Spirit of Christ".

Page 19 4A Emphasize the contrasting ideas "*good*" and "*sinful*".

4B In the second sentence emphasize the contrasting ideas "*bless*" and "*curse*". "*Bless*" is an old idea already expressed in the first sentence; but in the second sentence we're not emphasizing "*bless*" because it's a new idea, but because it contrasts with "*curse*". And the contrast must be made clear.

4C Emphasize the contrasting ideas "*physical*" and "*spiritual*".

4D Emphasize the contrasting ideas "*flock*" and "*fleece*".

4E Emphasize the contrasting ideas "*help*" and "*escort*".

Page 21 5A.A Emphasize the contrasting ideas "*difficult*" and "*easy*".
Emphasize the second contrasting ideas "*wrong*" and "*right*".

5A.B Emphasize the contrasting ideas "*nonsense*" and "*God's power*".
Emphasize the contrasting ideas "*lost*" and "*saved*".

5A.C In the second sentence emphasize the contrasting ideas "*don't do*" and "*do*".
Emphasize the contrasting ideas "*like*" and "*hate*".

5A.D Emphasize the contrasting ideas "*you*" and "*God*".
Emphasize the contrasting ideas "*others*" and "*you*".

5A.E Emphasize the contrasting ideas "*resists*" and "*gives grace*".
Emphasize the contrasting ideas "*proud*" and "*humble*".

Page 21 5B.A Emphasize the following contrasts:
"*obeys* them" and "does *not* obey them".
"*wise*" and "*foolish*".
"*rock*" and "*sand*".
"*not fall*" and "*fell*".

5B.B   Emphasize the following contrasts:
"*I*" and "*another*".
"*Father*" and "*self*-accredited".
"*no welcome*" and "*will* welcome".
"*me*" and "*him*".

Page 22 6A   First emphasize the contrasting ideas "*perishable*" and "*lasts*". Then emphasize the suggested contrast "*eternal*".

6B   Emphasize the suggested contrast "*him*". To *him* they are different, whereas to *us* they are the same.

Page 23 7A   Emphasize the contrasts "*I*" and "*you*", "*vine*" and "*branches*".

7B   Emphasize the contrasts "*we*" and "*he*", "*him*" and "*us*".

7C   Emphasize the contrasting ideas "*I*" and "*they*".

7D   Emphasize the contrasting ideas "*they*" and "*you and I*".

7E   Emphasize the contrasting ideas "*I*" and "*you*", "*them*" and "*me*".

7F   Emphasize the contrasting ideas "*he*" and "*I*", "*greater*" and "*less*".

Page 24 8A   Which days? "*Ignorant* days".

8B   Which beauty? "*Raving* beauty".
Which contest? "*Beauty* contest".
Don't forget to emphasize "*second*". It's a suggested contrast. *Second* rather than *first*.

8C   Which gods? "*Dumb heathen* gods".

8D   Which nature? "*Old sinful* nature".

8E   Which edition? "*First* edition". It's also a suggested contrast.

8F   What kind of saying? "*Trustworthy* saying".

Page 25 9A   Which things? "*All* things".

9B	"*Unclean* things".
9C	". . . the things they get for *nothing*".
9D	"*Sinful earthly* things".
9E	"*Some* things".
9F	"*Main* thing". "*Only* thing".
9G	"*All* things . . . things in *heaven* and on *earth*".
9H	"Things he'd *better not* do".
9I	"*Nice*" thing.
9J	"*Hardest* things".

Page 26 As well as any new ideas, emphasize the verbs that command.

10A	"*Close*".
10B	"*Repent*".
10C	"*Obey*".
10D	"*Leave . . . get . . .*"
10E	"*Go . . . tell . . . ask . . .*"

Page 26

11A	Subdue "When". Emphasize "*came*" or "*other*" depending on which might be the new idea.
11B	Subdue "When". Emphasize "*saw*" and "*getting out of hand*".
11C	Subdue "When". Emphasize "*realized*" and "*dead*".
11D	Subdue "When". Emphasize "*came*" and "*tomb*".
11E	Subdue "When". Emphasize "*taken*" and "*said*".

Page 27

12A	Subdue "which means Sent".
12B	Subdue "called the Twin".
12C	Subdue "who had gone to him before, and who was one of them".

Page 35

A	Pause before "who was full of grace and power".
B	Pause before "who speaks French".
C	Pause before "where he was brought up".
D	Pause before "who say there is no resurrection". It's a non-restricting phrase. All Sadducees did not believe in the resurrection.

The Importance of "Reading Out Loud"

In 1979 the Bible Society sponsored a research project into Bible use. The aim of the research was to find out more about the day-to-day use people made of the Bible. We wanted to obtain as broad a spectrum of answers as possible so we concentrated our attention on people who could be expected to have the opportunity for some regular contact with the Bible. Our sample was taken from Anglican and Nonconformist clergymen, church leaders and congregational members and we differentiated between their answers in our results. Part of the research was concerned with the Bible in public worship or the Bible for reading out loud. It also highlighted other ways in which worship could — and according to our sample should — be changed for the better.

Why we've published it

Our research has proved the need for this book because many people recognized the importance of public reading. They also saw the need for making it more effective through adequate training. We asked our respondents to describe their attitude to public Bible reading in church and found that nearly three-quarters of the people involved in the survey often enjoyed the reading in the service. This is a very important figure for us because we believe that if Bible readings are enjoyed in church, people will be encouraged to read their own Bibles at home. Dull readings may well discourage people from investigating the Bible more for themselves.

This is how the figures look:
13% thought that the reading was the highlight of the service
73% often enjoyed the reading
13% occasionally enjoyed the reading
1% rarely enjoyed the reading

Using "For Reading Out Loud" will help you to make sure that the people in your church will enjoy the Bible reading even more and will learn from it.

We discovered that the majority of the churches involved in our survey used readings of "medium length", that is of between ten and thirty verses. This means that if the passages are not well read, many people will miss a valuable opportunity of learning from the Bible. As "Reading Out Loud" says: "What you *see* as you read is the word of God, but what you read aloud, what you *say*, is *not necessarily* the word of God."

This need for good quality reading is emphasized by the fact that the majority of those involved in our survey — 53% — listen to the reading without following it in their own or a church Bible. Of the remainder, 19% follow the reading in a Bible provided by their church and 28% in their own copy. We believe that giving the members of the congregation the opportunity to read the passage as well as listen to it is vitally important. Our research shows that less than a third of the churches in the sample do supply Bibles. If many more churches were to provide Bibles it would encourage more people to follow the reading for themselves.

We also believe that, as "Reading Out Loud" points out, it is important that the version of the Bible to be read in church is appropriate to the members of the congregation who will hear it. The Bible Society has been involved in other research which shows that the more modern translations, and especially the GNB, are being bought more frequently than the older translations such as the AV, the RSV and the NEB. This trend mirrors the attitude of people involved in the study, because many people said that more modern versions should be used. The results of our question concerning reading the Bible out loud in church showed that nearly all the churches in our sample use or prefer one of the AV, RSV, NEB or GNB versions. The three leading versions used are the NEB (in 31% of the churches represented), the RSV (in 28%) and the GNB (in 19%).

Who it is for

"Reading Out Loud" is designed for everyone who is involved in public reading of the Bible. Many of our respondents said that they would like to see the laity more involved in public Bible reading in church. Although the Anglicans are beginning to do this, the trend is less noticeable among the Nonconformists and indeed more people could still be involved in all denominations. This book can help bring this about by teaching everyone to read God's word aloud effectively.

In our survey we found that while in 84% of Anglican churches the Bible is regularly read by "ordinary" church members, only in 48% of Nonconformist churches do members regularly take part in Bible reading. Conversely, in 95% of Nonconformist churches the clergy regularly read the Bible whereas in only 75% of Anglican churches is this true.

Other ways to improve the use of the Bible in public worship

Many people involved in the church have already begun to work at improving ways in which the Bible is read and used in church services. Here are some of their suggestions:

○ Readers should really believe and understand the passage that they are reading — one of the points emphasized in "Reading Out Loud". (Here the use of study aids is very important. Write to the Bible Society for a catalogue of our range.)

○ An introduction to, or a summary of, the passage might be helpful.

○ A silence should be left after the reading to allow the message to sink in.

○ The passage should be read through twice.

○ Advance notice of the readings is very important.

Other comments included pleas for experimentation with ways of presenting the Bible (e.g. drama, dialogue).

We hope that these results will show you that reading the Bible out loud is a regular church event that can, and should, be made into a vivid and exciting part of every service.

The Bible on cassette

For an excellent example of how to read the Bible in public listen to the Good News Bible cassettes produced by the Bible Society. These show how to emphasize, pause and phrase, to give correct meaning and easy, enjoyable listening. Send for details to
Bible Society,
146, Queen Victoria Street,
LONDON EC4V 4BX.